Spotlight on
ANCIENT CIVILIZATIONS
GREECE

Ancient Greek GOVERNMENT

Henry Bensinger

Published in 2014 by The Rosen Publishing Group, Inc.
29 East 21st Street, New York, NY 10010

First Edition

Editor: Joanne Randolph
Book Design: Kate Vlachos

Photo Credits: Cover Tatiana Popova/Shutterstock.com; p. 4 Michael Schmeling/Getty Images; p. 5 Andrey Starostin; p. 6 Nick K./Shutterstock.com; p. 7 Education Images/UIG/Universal Images Group/Getty Images; pp. 8, 19 Hulton Archive/Stringer/Hulton Archive/Getty Images; p. 9 Danita Delimont/Gallo Images/Getty Images; p. 10 Universal Images Group/Getty Images; p. 11 Anastasios71/Shutterstock.com; p. 13 Nick Pavlakis/Shutterstock.com; p. 14 Antonio Abrignani/Shutterstock.com; p. 15 © imagebroker.net/SuperStock; p. 17 St.Leggio/Shutterstock.com; p. 18 bkp/Shutterstock.com; p. 20 DEA/G. Dagli Orti/De Agostini Picture Library/Getty Images; p. 21 pavalena/Shutterstock.com; p. 22 Renata Sedmakova/Shutterstock.com.

Library of Congress Cataloging-in-Publication Data

Bensinger, Henry.
Ancient Greek government / by Henry Bensinger. — First edition.
pages cm. — (Spotlight on ancient civilizations: Greece)
Includes index.
ISBN 978-1-4777-0770-8 (library binding) — ISBN 978-1-4777-0873-6 (pbk.) — ISBN 978-1-4777-0874-3 (6-pack)
1. Greece—Civilization—To 146 B.C.—Juvenile literature. I. Title.
DF77.B528 2014
320.938—dc23

2012049556

Manufactured in the United States of America

CPSIA Compliance Information: Batch #S13PK2: For Further Information contact Rosen Publishing, New York, New York at 1-800-237-9932

CONTENTS

Always Changing

The people of ancient Greece shared many things. They spoke the same language. They believed in the same myths and gods. They had many of the same **traditions**. They also thought of themselves as Greek.

MAP OF MAJOR GREEK CITY-STATES

Greece has many mountains, so neighboring city-states did not have much contact with one another. This is why city-states developed their own identities and separate systems of government. These are the ruins of the Temple of Apollo in the city-state of Corinth.

However, all the towns and cities of Greece, called city-states, had their own special identities. Greeks were proud of their city-states. Each city-state had its own government, laws, and customs. Around 700 BC, most of the city-states were **oligarchies**. An oligarchy is a system of government in which a small number of rich, powerful men rule a larger group of people.

The Most Famous Oligarchy

One of the most powerful oligarchies of ancient Greece was Sparta. The men of Sparta were known for being skilled soldiers. Sparta had two kings, who were also the leaders of the army.

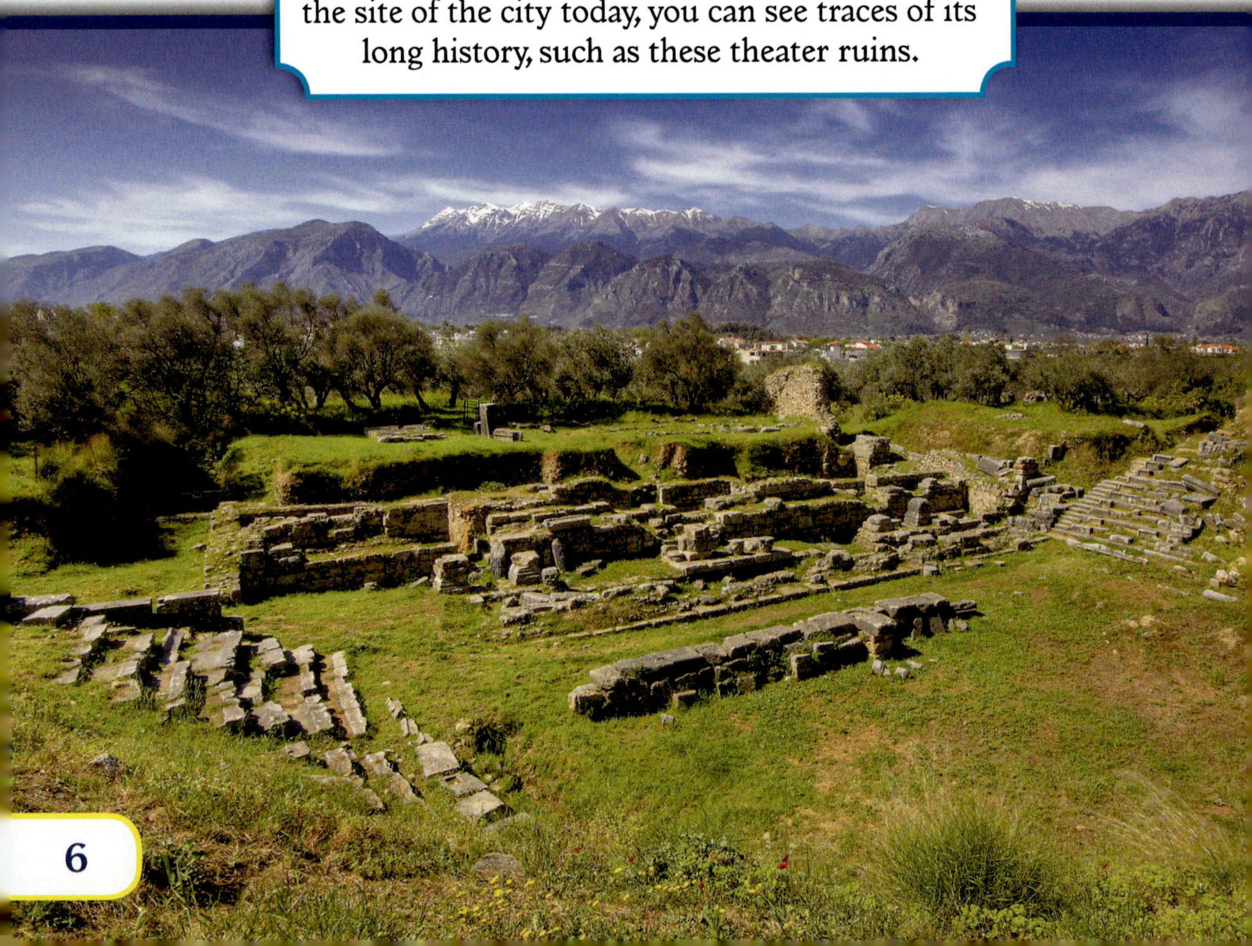

Sparta was founded around 900 BC. If you visit the site of the city today, you can see traces of its long history, such as these theater ruins.

This modern statue is of King Leonidas of Sparta. In 480 BC, Leonidas and other Spartans died defending Greece against the Persians at the Battle of Thermopylae.

Sparta's kings were part of a council, called the *gerousia*. It also included 28 elders, who were **elected** by the **citizens** of Sparta to serve for life. An **assembly** made up of adult male Spartan citizens voted on plans suggested by the gerousia.

Sparta also had a group of five powerful magistrates, called ephors. Ephors were elected to serve for one year. They carried out laws passed by the gerousia.

Tyranny

Oligarchies were not always well liked by the citizens of ancient Greece. They did not like that a small group of people made all the decisions. Wealthy people often became wealthier by taking land and money away from poor farmers. Sometimes the people would rise up and **rebel** against the government.

Gelon was a tyrant who ruled Gela and, later, Syracuse. Both were Greek city-states located in what is now Italy.

Periander was the tyrant of the Greek city-state of Corinth between about 628 and 588 BC. This is a Roman copy of a Greek statue of Periander from the fourth century BC.

These rebellions made it easy for a powerful person to take control. These powerful people were called **tyrants,** and they ruled by force. They took land and money and sometimes killed people who stood against them. The people liked tyrants even less than they liked oligarchies. Tyrants would eventually be thrown out, too, and the oligarchy system would return. The ancient Greeks needed a new system!

Solon and Athens

Solon passed reforms that helped Athens's economy grow. Trade grew and Athenian goods, such as this vase from around 530 BC, became popular across the Greek world.

Greece did not find a new system until the sixth century BC. Around 594 BC, the people of Athens decided they needed a change. They wanted the people to have a voice in the government. This kind of government is called a **democracy**. The people of Athens elected Solon to be their leader.

Democracy did not last long at first. After Solon died, a tyrant took over. Then, Cleisthenes became the leader in Athens in 507 BC. He gave all male citizens the right to vote, freedom of speech, and lots of other new rights. Democracy was taking hold!

These are the remains of the agora in Athens. The agora was the place where citizens came together to vote on laws. It also served as the marketplace.

Democracy Rules

Other city-states followed Athens's example and changed their governments to democracies. The word "democracy" comes from the Greek words *demos*, which means "people," and *kratos*, which means "rule."

In these democracies, the citizens elected officials, such as judges and generals. They sometimes used a lottery system to pick citizens to do other government jobs. A citizen might be chosen to be a prison guard or the town treasurer under this system.

Citizens were freemen who had been born in Greece. Slaves and outsiders were not considered citizens. Citizens could own land, vote, serve in the army, and speak in court.

The Acropolis and the Parthenon, in Athens, have become symbols for Athenian democracy, culture, and ideas. The Acropolis Restoration Project has worked to restore the buildings since 1975.

The Assembly

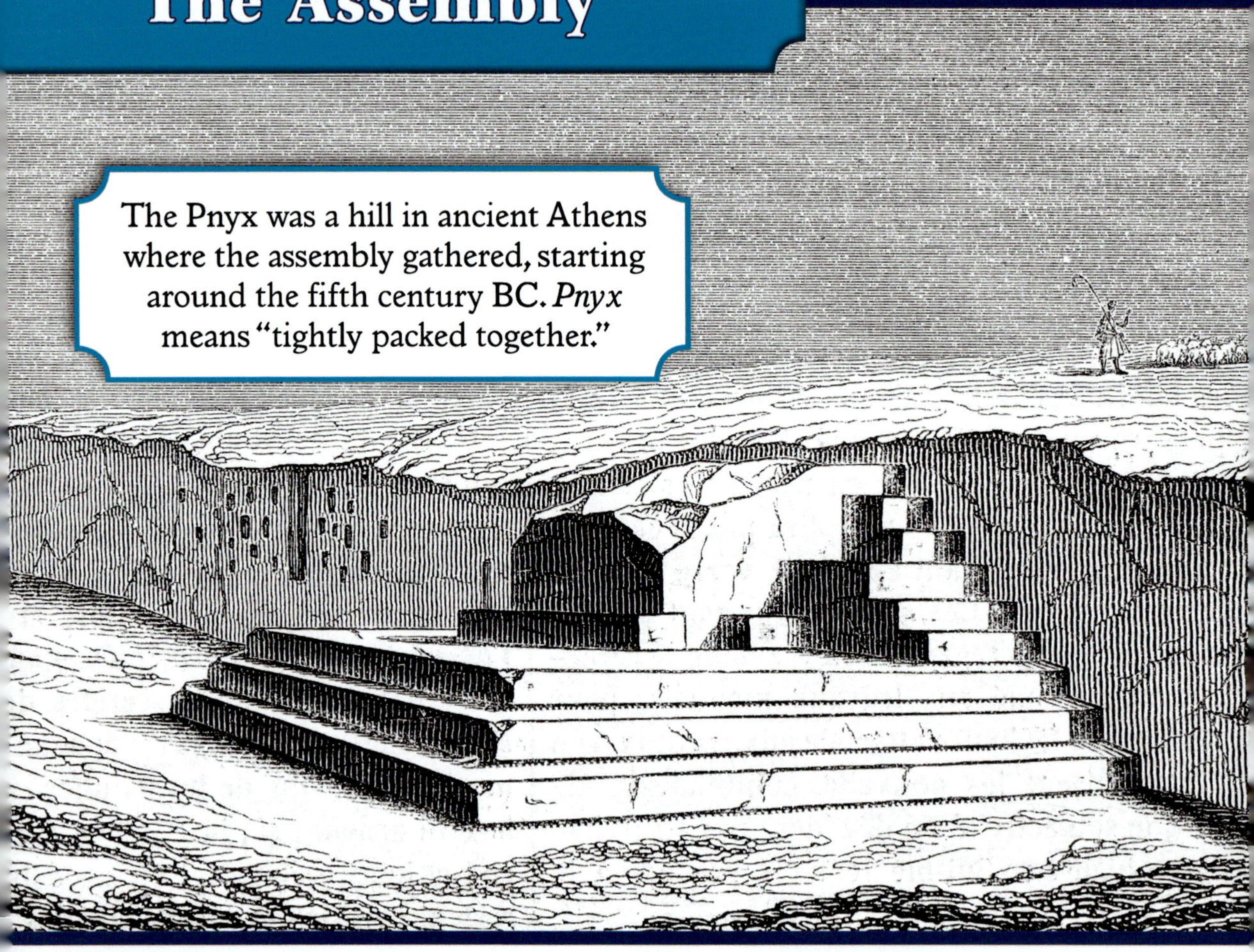

The Pnyx was a hill in ancient Athens where the assembly gathered, starting around the fifth century BC. *Pnyx* means "tightly packed together."

When citizens of ancient Greece gathered to vote or discuss issues of government, the gathering was called the assembly. At first, the assembly met once a month. Later, though, the assembly met three to four times a month. Citizens had to attend the meeting in order to vote.

It was a citizen's right to attend the assembly. It was also considered a duty. The assembly met to vote on whether or not to go to war. It also met to elect certain officials. Its other main job was to settle political crimes.

These ruins of an assembly room are in Crete. Most of what we know about the assemblies in Greece comes from Athens, but other Greek city-states had them as well.

The Boule

One of the jobs of the assembly was to elect the boule. The boule was a council of citizens who ran the daily activities of the city-state. In some city-states, the boule served as the court of law. It heard cases and made decision on laws when the assembly was not meeting. As time went on, the boule also took over decisions regarding trade, slavery, the military, construction, and much more.

While most city-states had boules, Sparta did not. However, the gerousia, or council of elders, played a similar role there.

The place where the boule met was called a bouleuterion. These are the ruins of the bouleuterion in Akrai, a Greek settlement in what is now Italy.

The Military

The people of ancient Greece fought in many wars. The city-states fought against each other. They also fought against **foreign** lands. Most of the Greek city-states required their male citizens between the ages of 20 and 60 to serve as part-time soldiers. If there was a war, all citizens were required to fight.

This is a Spartan helmet. Sparta was known for having the best soldiers in ancient Greece.

This Greek vase from the fifth century BC shows a fight between cavalry and infantry. Cavalry fight on horseback and infantry fight on foot. Greek armies used both, but infantry played a bigger role.

The rules in Sparta were different from those in the rest of Greece. The military was the heart of their government. Boys left home to train in military school at the age of 7. When they reached the age of 20, they could fight in wars. Spartan warriors trained throughout their lives.

Athens and Sparta at Odds

While Sparta was building its military, Athens developed a rich culture that focused on learning, the arts, and philosophy. The differences between these two powerful city-states eventually led to war between them. This war was called the Peloponnesian War, which was fought between 431 and 404 BC.

This carving shows Athenian hoplites. Hoplites were soldiers who usually marched on foot and carried shields and spears.

MAP OF ALLIES IN THE PELOPONNESIAN WAR

This map shows the areas that were allies of Sparta and Athens in the Peloponnesian War. Allies are people or groups who fight on the same side.

Both sides gathered allies and support from other city-states. The fighting went on for decades and brought with it many hardships. There were **famines**, **plagues**, and many deaths. Athens lost in the end, but neither city-state remained as powerful after the war.

The Men Who Ruled the Land

Ancient Greek civilization has had a lasting impact on today's world. In part, this is due to the ideas of the men who ruled the ancient Greek city-states, especially Athens. Solon worked to change the government into a democracy. Pericles also promoted democracy. He led Athens for around 30 years.

Alexander of Macedon, also called Alexander the Great, was a Greek king. He took over lands throughout Persia and into Africa. Many of these places adopted Greek culture and ideas.

Pericles promoted the arts and began the building of the Parthenon and other buildings on the Acropolis.

GLOSSARY

assembly (uh-SEM-blee) A group of people who meet to advise a government.

citizens (SIH-tih-zenz) People who were born in or have a right to live in a country or other community.

democracy (dih-MAH-kruh-see) A government that is run by the people who live under it.

elected (ee-LEK-tid) Chosen for an office by voters.

famines (FA-menz) Shortages of food that cause people to go hungry.

foreign (FOR-in) Outside one's own country.

oligarchies (AH-lih-gar-keez) Systems of government in which a small number of people hold the power over the larger group.

plagues (PLAYGZ) Very bad illnesses, curses, or hardships.

rebel (rih-BEL) To disobey the people or country in charge.

traditions (truh-DIH-shunz) Ways of doing things that have been passed down over time.

tyrants (TY-rints) Mean rulers.

INDEX

WEBSITES

Due to the changing nature of Internet links, PowerKids Press has developed an online list of websites related to the subject of this book. This site is updated regularly. Please use this link to access the list: www.powerkidslinks.com/sacg/gov/